*T*HE EXPERT GUIDE

To

Dating Victorian Family Photographs

CONTENTS

INTRODUCTION

The daguerreotype was the first photographic process which lent itself to commercial exploitation. Details of the process were published in France in January 1939. By March 1841 the first commercial daguerreotype studio in Britain had opened its doors in London's Regent Street. In 1851 Frederick Scott Archer published details of a new process, the so-called wet collodion process, that was to lay the foundation for future directions in photography. It heralded the death of the daguerreotype. The major article of commerce in the decade of the 1850s was a modification of Archer's process known as the wet collodion positive. This converted a glass negative into a positive which was then placed into a case or frame similar to those used for daguerreotypes.

So far, so good. Dating in these early years is considerably assisted by simple identification of process and format. From 1860 to the end of the century, however, two variations of the card format came to dominate the market. The card formats worked on the basic principle of pasting a positive paper print cut to a standard size onto a cardboard mount which had also been cut to a standard size. Following its popularity in France, the carte de visite, the first of the major card formats, made its debut on the high street in Britain in the spring of 1860. It was to remain in circulation until the postcard format of the early twentieth century eventually displaced it. (Since the postcard format was not introduced into commercial portrait photography until c1902, it is not included in this survey.) 1866 saw the introduction of the carte's big sister, the so-called cabinet format. The cabinet was simply a larger version of the carte. Together the carte de visite and the cabinet formed the backbone of the Victorian Family Album. Because they dominated the market for fifty years or more, the dating of Victorian card photographs can prove difficult for specialist and amateur alike.

THE EXPERT GUIDE

To

Dating Victorian Family Photographs

By

Audrey Linkman

GREATER MANCHESTER COUNTY RECORD OFFICE
2000

$\mathcal{P}$REFACE

If you thought that the dress of the sitter offered the only means of dating Victorian Family Photographs, then this *Expert Guide* is the book for you! Of course, dress is a valuable aid in dating, but there are other equally important elements of early photographic portraits which provide clues and pointers. This publication looks in detail at some of these, particularly those associated with the make-up and physical appearance of the photograph and its mount. *The Expert Guide to Dating Victorian Family Photographs* is designed to address the needs of genealogists and social historians. It will also prove very useful to archivists, librarians and museum curators and all those charged with the care and interpretation of the photographic record.

The present work is intended as the first of a series of Expert Guides which will explore different aspects of early photographs and their value as historical records. Future publications will feature Victorian Studio Portraits and their Interpretation, and the Itinerant Tradition in Victorian Portrait Photography.

If you have any queries or comments about the contents of the present volume, please contact the author, c/o The Documentary Photography Archive, 7 Towncroft Lane, Bolton BL1 5EW. Tel/Fax: 01204 840439.

This publication has been funded by the Greater Manchester County Record Office. The author would like to express her grateful thanks to the Archivist and his staff for their kind assistance and support.

The Documentary Photography Archive and the Greater Manchester County Record Office are working together to establish the Record Office as a Centre of Specialism in the photographic record.

It is an error to assume that the dating of early photographs is solely dependent on the information contained in the image itself. Many people, for example, assume that a knowledge of fashion and particularly female dress is the most important element in determining a date. This is not the case. Indeed in dating head and shoulders vignette portraits where detail shades off into a plain background, close examination of the cardboard mount can reveal much more information than can be gleaned from the image. Of course, image content plays a role in dating, but photohistorians pay particular attention to factors such as the style and physical appearance of the cardboard mount; written information, both printed and manuscript, which features on the cardboard mount; and the photographic process used in the production of the print. All of these elements are taken into the evaluation in order to arrive at a possible dating.

Even so, it may only be possible to date a photograph to a decade or suggest a possible three to five year span. Specific dating to the year of production will normally prove the exception rather than the rule. It is surprising to realise how few business records or back files of negatives survive from the studios and portrait parlours that dotted the high street in Victorian Britain. It is perhaps also worth mentioning that the details and dates given here apply to developments in Britain, and possibly connect closely with the history of commercial photography in countries in the Empire. However, the pattern of photography's commercial development in other countries such as France or America was distinctive and different.

DATING BY FORMAT

2.1 DAGUERREOTYPES 1841 - c 1855

Daguerreotype images were made directly onto a copper plate which carried a thin coating of silver. No negative was involved in the process. The silver surface of the plate was polished to ensure fine detail and then sensitised by fumes from iodine and bromine. After exposure in the camera, the latent image was developed by holding the plate over fumes of mercury. It was then fixed with hypo. It was usual to gild the image with a solution of gold salt to give a warmer tone to the finished photograph. Many daguerreotype portraits are delicately coloured. The paint was applied by hand after the process was complete. Some miniature painters, whose livelihood was threatened by the invention of the camera, took up photography; many others found work hand colouring the new photographs. (See Plate 1)

PLATE 1. PHOTOGRAPHER UNKNOWN
Portrait of a seated woman. c1850. Cased daguerreotype. Author's Collection.
The woman's face has been delicately blushed with pink. The case is covered with red leather and lined with velvet.

The surface of the daguerreotype plate was extremely fragile, easy to scratch and quick to tarnish. For protection the plate was covered with glass and sealed with a paper binding. Frequently a gilt mount was inserted between plate and glass, serving to enhance the overall appearance and keep the two apart.

The daguerreotype could then be placed either in a frame, usually papier maché, suitable for hanging on a wall; or bound in a narrow gilt frame and fitted into a case, similar to those previously used to house hand-painted portrait miniatures. The most common cases were made of wood covered with dark red leather. The inside of the lid was usually lined with red plush. "Union Cases" imported from America are also found. (See under collodion positives).

Daguerreotypes generally were fairly small, the most popular sizes measuring 2½ x 3¼ inches and 2¾ x 3¼ inches. Costs varied according to size, mountings and, indeed, date of production. Colouring was usually charged extra. In 1841 the cheapest daguerreotype retailed at one guinea. By 1845/46 in Leeds, for example, this had fallen to ten shillings and sixpence, and by 1852 to seven shillings. Nonetheless the daguerreotype in Britain remained a luxury article, the preserve of the wealthy.

The major distinguishing feature of the daguerreotype is its ability, when gently moved in different directions, to fluctuate between a negative and positive appearance as it reflects light from different angles. Another characteristic is its tendency to exhibit blue tarnishing around the edges of the plate where airborne pollutants have managed to penetrate the casing.

The first daguerreotype studio was opened in Britain on the roof of the Royal Polytechnic Institution, Regent Street, London, on 23 March 1841 by the patent speculator Richard Beard. Through the intervention of the French government, the daguerreotype process could be practised freely throughout the world. Only in England, Wales and the colonies was it subject to patent restriction. This patent restriction added to the costs of opening a photographic business. Beard licensed a number of studios throughout Britain in the 1840s. Licensees tended to favour towns and cities which boasted sufficient numbers of wealthy inhabitants to sustain a remunerative level of business. The first Lancashire studio opened in Mount Gardens, St James Walk, Liverpool in October 1841, and the first Manchester studio in Ducie Place at the back of the Exchange in November 1841.

By the mid 1840s we get reports of unlicensed itinerants visiting towns, establishing temporary studios, and remaining as long as business warranted before moving on to fresh pastures. These itinerants were respectable in the sense that they served a high-class clientele and charged relatively high prices. One such itinerant, John Beattie, claimed to have totally given up the daguerreotype process and converted to collodion in 1855. John Werge, another early itinerant, had abandoned the daguerreotype entirely by 1857. By October 1858, *The Photographic News* could confidently announce that "The daguerreotype process is so little used now, that we doubt if a series of articles on it would be of any interest to the bulk of our readers."

2.2 WET COLLODION POSITIVES OR AMBROTYPES 1852 - c 1890

In March 1851 Frederick Scott Archer published details of a new photographic process which employed glass as the support for the photographic negative. A clean glass plate was first coated with a mixture of collodion and potassium iodide, and then sensitised by a second coating of silver nitrate. The plate had to be exposed in the camera while this silver nitrate coating was still wet, since the negative lost its sensitivity as it dried - hence the name of wet collodion process. Immediately after exposure the glass negative was developed, fixed and washed. (See Plate 2)

PLATE 2. PHOTOGRAPHERS UNKNOWN
Above: *Portrait of a young woman holding opera glasses.* c1855.
Below: *Portrait of a woman.* c1860.
These two cased portraits illustrate the difference in quality between collodion positives produced in the 1850s. The top portrait has jewellery details picked out in gold paint and is housed in a fine Union Case. Author's Collection.

In 1852 Archer published a variation of the process whereby the negative was effectively turned into a positive. This involved the simple process of bleaching the negative with nitric acid or bichloride of mercury. On backing the glass with black paper or black velvet or simply coating the back with black varnish, the photograph appeared positive. The glass photograph was then placed behind a sheet of clear glass and fitted in frames and cases similar to those used to house daguerreotypes. A new style of casing decorated with finely detailed designs reached Britain from America in the mid 1850s. Known as "Union Cases", these were produced by pressing a heated mixture of finely ground sawdust, shellac and colour into a steel die. When cold this mixture set hard retaining all the details of the die. The process was patented by Samuel Peck of New Haven, Connecticut, on 3 October 1854. Many of the Union cases found in Britain were imported from America, but recent evidence has revealed the existence of British manufacturers. See John Hannavy, British Union Case Makers, *Photographica World*, No.91 (Winter 1999/2000), pp.35-43.

The wet collodion positive boasted a number of variants. The so-called Relievo process was introduced in 1854 by the Glasgow photographer, John Urie. The background to the portrait was scraped away or the sitter was photographed against a plain, dark ground. In Relievo negatives only the back of the figure was painted black, and the whole of the negative was subsequently placed against a white, coloured or painted backing paper. This made the detailed figure appear to stand out against the light background. The Ambrotype was a variant suggested by James Cutting in 1854 in which the cover glass was sealed to the plate by Canada Balsam. Ambrotype is the name most commonly used for collodion positives in America but the title was never used in Britain at the time of the process's popularity.

The collodion positive was the major article of commerce in Britain in the second half of the 1850s. The collodion process was certainly cheaper than the daguerreotype. In the 1840s Thomas Sutton paid thirty pounds for a complete daguerreotype apparatus. By December 1853 a complete apparatus for collodion was advertised at four guineas. Collodion was also simpler, especially the collodion positive process, as this involved no complex printing procedures. Instruction manuals flooded onto the market. In addition, following a court case heard in December 1854, all patent restrictions surrounding photography in Britain were finally removed. As a result more people turned to photography as a means of making money and earning a living. In London, the dozen or so photographers listed in the trade directories in 1851 had swollen to sixty six in 1855. By 1857 the numbers had increased to a staggering one hundred and fifty five.

When it first appeared on the market the wet collodion positive retailed at ten shillings and sixpence, half the initial retail price of the smallest daguerreotype. However, with rapidly escalating competition prices fell steadily throughout the 1850s until, by the end of the decade, the cheap portrait parlour had made its appearance. By 1857 glass positives were widely advertised at one shilling and a year later prices had fallen to sixpence (case twopence extra!). By means of their pricing policy studios now began to target specific sectors of the market. The decade that had opened with the luxury daguerreotype closed with the sixpenny glass positive. For the first time in Britain working people could afford to have their photograph taken.

Certain photographers in the 1850s who worked at the exclusive end of the market refused to deal in glass positives. They claimed that the glass positive lacked the delicacy of the daguerreotype. They may also have wished to preserve prices at a level which distinguished the exclusive practitioner from the rest. Instead, they offered their high class clientele portraits printed on paper from wet collodion glass negatives. These portraits were usually overpainted in monochrome on the surface of the print, or finished in water-colours. These paper portraits commanded good prices, the whole plate size, approximately eight inches by six, costing from two guineas upwards.

Nonetheless, good quality glass positives continued to be produced from growing numbers of studios throughout the 1850s. Then came the sudden, swift invasion of the carte de visite in the early 1860s and within a couple of years the glass positive was effectively banished from respectable ateliers on the high street. Happily, however, the glass positive continued in production, but in a very different context. From the late 1850s to the 1890s cheap glass positives were produced by itinerant photographers who went from door to door in search of speculative work, or trundled hand carts onto the beach, pitched booths in the fairground or set up shop al fresco in parks, commons and local beauty spots. For this class of operator the glass positive had a distinctive advantage - it could be produced "while you wait" i.e. within a matter of some five minutes or so. The quality of these products, with regard both to the portraits and their cases, is generally poorer than in work dating to the 1850s. (See Plate 3)

PLATE 3. PHOTOGRAPHER UNKNOWN
Man and woman on the sands.
A handwritten label pasted onto the verso of this photograph reads: Mr George Thorne, designer of
the Oakhampton railway bridge and a native of Barnstaple, North Devon. May 1864.
Wet collodion positive in cheap frame. Author's Collection.

2.3 FERROTYPES or TINTYPES c 1855 - c 1930s

The ferrotype was produced in much the same way as the glass positive except that a thin sheet of iron coated with black enamel was used in place of the glass. The idea occurred to several people in the 1850s, but it was not until the first ferrotype patent in the United States was granted to Hamilton L. Smith in 1856 that the process achieved widespread commercial success. Very few ferrotypes were produced in Britain in the 1850s, though the process had achieved widespread popularity in America by the 1860s. In August 1871, the American Phoenix Plate Company obtained a patent on the "chocolate" or tinted plate in England. They sent agents across the Atlantic to introduce the plate, but they arrived late in the season and little was done. Early in 1872, Thomas Sherman Estabrooke, one of the best known ferrotypers in America, accepted the agency of the Phoenix Plate Co. in England and proceeded to London in June to establish in Regent Street the first gallery in this country devoted exclusively to the production of ferrotypes. During the 1870s in Britain a small number of studios introduced the format offering quarterplate, i.e. four by three inch ferrotype plates at sixpence each to a largely working class clientele. (See Plate 4) The plates could be inserted into paper frames but these frequently disintegrate over time.

A cheap ferrotype novelty appeared on the market at the very end of the 1870s. Retailing at nine for seven and a half pence, these were known as "American Gems" or "Gem" portraits. They comprised a postage stamp size ferrotype plate inserted into a carte de visite style cardboard mount which carried a tiny oval aperture. (See Plate 5) The face of the mount was usually decorated with some sort of printed pattern or an embossed design around the opening. Packaged in this way Gems could readily be inserted in the photographic album. The Gem also had a larger sister known as the Victoria. Victoria plates measured approximately $2^{1}/_{4}$ x $1^{3}/_{4}$ inches and these, too, were inserted in carte de visite size card mounts. Victorias retailed at three for one shilling.

These tiny portraits were produced using multilens cameras. A camera fitted with nine lenses, for example, could take nine pictures at one exposure. After processing the tinplate was simply cut with scissors to provide the multiple copies which would otherwise be impracticable in a process involving no negative. American Gems were the cheapest photographs on the market and were produced "while you wait". These were the first style of ferrotype to enjoy any measure of popularity on the high street in Britain. Some firms specialised in ferrotype and gem work. Two of the best known were those of James Frederick Lowrie and Joshua Jewell who established branches throughout the country in the early 1880s. Local photographers who served the popular end of the market offered gems and ferrotypes in addition to cartes and cabinets. Superior establishments courting an exclusive clientele would never dream of having any contact with this product.

PLATE 4. ESTABROOKE, 57, Oxford Street, London.
Portrait of a young woman in chequered dress. 1870s. Ferrotype. 10.1 x 6.1cms. Author's Collection.
Fine quality ferrotype of a young woman, her cheeks delicately blushed with pink. Note the detail in
the bottom left corner showing the back of her dress from the neighbouring picture.
A printed label pasted on the verso of this plate reads: Estabrooke's American Ferrotypes.
From one to eight cards, in different positions, taken at a sitting, finished and delivered in 15 minutes.
57 Oxford Street, 3 doors west of Berners St. London. Old Pictures Copied.

PLATE 5. J. JEWELL, 41 Gra(i)nger Street, Newcastle on Tyne, Liverpool & Manchester. **Head and shoulders portrait of a lady.** c1881. American Gem Ferrotype. Author's Collection. A typical example showing the recto and verso of this style of portrait. The postage stamp size ferrotype is held in place by a paper cover pasted over the back of the mount. This paper cover shows faint signs of rust. The use of a stamp for the Newcastle address suggests that this branch has only recently opened. The misspelling of Grainger Street does not project an image of careful attention to detail in the studio!

Ferrotypes, however, were most popular with itinerant photographers who worked at the seaside, in the fairground or at the roadside. (See Plate 6) Because it was lighter, cheaper and less fragile than glass, the ferrotype quickly ousted the collodion positive as the favourite "instant" format. Ferrotype dry plates (i.e. commercially produced and ready sensitised) appeared on the market in 1891. These were followed by the introduction of cameras with built-in processing facilities which obviated the need for portable darkboxes in which to sensitise and process. These innovations extended the life of the ferrotype. Ferrotype photographers were still working the beaches in the 1930s and one, at least, was operating in the streets of London as late as the 1950s.

The ferrotype plate was sometimes placed in a papier maché frame or inserted into a paper slip or mounted on card. Frequently today they are found loose and as such are easy to identify. Those in frames are sometimes difficult to distinguish from glass positives. Look for evidence of rust "blisters" on the surface of the image. Rust marks also appear on backing paper in the case of those in slips or card mounts. A magnet can prove useful in some cases.

More detailed information about the ferrotype is available in Audrey Linkman, Cheap Tin Trade: The Ferrotype Portrait in Victorian Britain, *Photographica World*, No.69 (June 1994), pp.17-28.

PLATE 6. PHOTOGRAPHER UNKNOWN.
Three women and a man at the seaside. 1890s. Ferrotype plate. Author's Collection.
This little group of four appear to be posing for their picture beside a bathing machine.

2.4   CARD FORMATS

The card formats heralded the arrival of the mass market in commercial portrait photography. Mass production could be achieved by making multiple exposures on a single negative. In the case of the carte de visite as many as eight small portraits could be printed from a single glass negative. These were then cut to a standard size and mounted on cards of a standard size. The commercial success of the carte was such that for the rest of the century photographers tried to repeat a Golden Age of massive sales and soaring profits by introducing variations of size on the card format theme. However, only the carte de visite and the cabinet ever achieved widespread, lasting popularity.

Those requiring further information about the various other card formats introduced in the nineteenth century should consult: Audrey Linkman, Nineteenth Century Card Formats in Britain, *Royal Photographic Society Historical Group Supplement*, No. 92 (March 1991).

This method of working lent itself particularly to the mass production of portraits of celebrities and public figures for the commercial market. Carte portraits of the nationally and locally famous could be purchased at print shops, stationers, fancy goods and novelty emporia and even from vendors in the street. These were housed in the album along with photographs of family and friends. Since many of these photographs carried no identification they can easily be mistaken for family portraits.

In the case of private commissions the new format required the public to purchase in quantity what they had hitherto been accustomed to buy as single items. The purpose-designed album was therefore introduced together with the carte de visite in the early 1860s to encourage the public to amass collections of photographs through gift and exchange. The card format and the photo album proved a winning formula which appealed to the public and kept us coming back to the photographer for new portraits to add to our growing collections of family photographs.

2.5 CARTES DE VISITE 1860 - c 1910

In November 1854 a young Paris-based photographer André Adolphe Eugene Disdéri patented the carte de visite. His patent enshrined the concept of creating a number of small size negatives on one large negative plate, so that by a single process of developing and printing multiple copies of prints could be produced. A camera fitted with four identical lenses and a repeating back mechanism could thus produce eight tiny images on a single negative plate. After development the prints could be cut to a standard size (usually 2⅛ x 3½ inches) and pasted onto cardboard mounts manufactured to a standard size (usually 2½ x 4 inches).

The carte de visite was first advertised for sale in Britain in the spring of 1860 and continued in circulation beyond the turn of the century. Throughout that period a number of variations on the basic carte format were introduced. These included:

Medallion portraits comprise one or more, tiny oval prints measuring approximately 1 x ¾ inch, which were pasted into the carte de visite mount. They are usually surrounded by a delicate printed design. They came onto the market in 1863.

The **Diamond Cameo** appeared in 1864. This features 4 tiny portraits each showing different views of the sitter's face. (See Plate 7) These bust portraits measuring 1 x ¾ inch are arranged in a diamond shape on the carte mount and this feature gives the style its name. The top and bottom portrait generally show a front face view and a three-quarter view; the others, two entire profiles, or a profile of one side and a five eighths view of the other, though variation is possible. Unlike the simple medallions, the oval containing each portrait was punched into relief so as to present a convex surface. This style was patented by its designer, F.R. Window, and a licence mark frequently appears on the mount. Photographers prepared to purchase the patent rights were usually situated at the expensive/exclusive end of the market. Diamond Cameos were relatively expensive compared to other styles of carte de visite. In 1865, for example, the Exeter photographer Brice advertised his prices as follows: Diamond Cameo cartes 15s dozen; Medallion cartes in four positions, 7/6d dozen; Ordinary cartes 10/6d per doz. Vignetted cartes at 12s dozen.

Quinque Gems were a modification of the diamond cameo proposed in 1865 by the photographer John Palmer of Stonehouse in Devon.

The **Bi-Medallion** or **Doublet** first appeared in 1870. The style was devised by H.C. Lee of Blaenavon. It consists of a couple of oval medallions side by side, and in contact. The medallion portraits often feature a husband and wife, or two views of the same sitter. (See Plate 8)

PLATE 7. JAMES MUDD, Manchester.
Four head and shoulders portraits of a young man. c1864.
Diamond Cameo carte de visite. Author's Collection.
Note the licence mark at the centre of the base of the mount. The careful and different positioning of
each of the four heads is also typical in these portraits.

18

PLATE 8. W. & D. DOWNEY,
9 Eldon Square, Newcastle on Tyne and
61 Ebury Street, London.
Princess Louise and the Marquis of Lorne. c1871.
Bi-Medallion or Doublet carte de visite. Author's Collection.
Princess Louise, the fourth daughter of Victoria and Albert, married John, Marquis of Lorne (later ninth Duke of Argyll) in 1871. The word "copyright" in the bottom right corner suggests that the firm of Downey published this carte for the commercial market about the time of the engagement or marriage. As this style first appeared in 1870 its association with Royal subjects will have served to promote its acceptance with the public.

The **Cameo Medallion Vignette** style first appeared in Italy in 1870 and was produced in Britain from 1871. The carte features a large vignetted head and bust in an oval mask which was pressed in an oval convex die. The background in the oval shaped vignette contrasts in tone with the shade of the surrounding border, so that the portrait really does appear to stand out like a cameo. This style enjoyed some degree of popularity throughout the period and is frequently found in the family album. The photographers, Vandyke and Brown of Liverpool, proposed to charge five shillings more per dozen for cameo vignettes than for ordinary cartes. (See Plate 9)

PLATE 9. VANDYKE & BROWN, 31 Bold Street, 34 Castle Street, 87 Lord Street, Liverpool.
Head and shoulders vignette of an adult male. c1872.
Cameo Medallion Vignette carte de visite. Author's Collection.
It is not surprising that this lovely style remained popular throughout the period.

The **Triptographic Cameo** appeared in 1872 devised by Mr Nicholls of Cambridge. It features a larger oval medallion in the centre of the carte flanked on either side by a smaller one. (See Plate 10)

The **Triplet** features three poses of the same individual on the same carte and was proposed by Mr Anckorn in 1884.

PLATE 10. HENRY A. CHAPMAN, Swansea.
Three head and shoulders portraits of a young woman. c1872.
Triptographic Cameo carte de visite. Author's Collection.
Note how the larger portrait in the centre shows the young lady wearing her hat. In the two smaller pictures flanking the main portrait, her hat has been removed.

Cartes de visite featuring a **rectangular shaped convex portrait** made an appearance on the scene from c1878. Unfortunately the editorial sections of the trade journals made no reference to the introduction of this style so its contemporary title remains as yet a mystery. (See Plate 11)

PLATE 11. THOMAS MILLER, Midland Road, Wellingborough.
Threequarter view of man wearing mortar board. c1880.
Rectangular Convex carte de visite. Author's Collection.
Like the cameo medallion this is a style which continued to be produced in relatively small numbers to the end of the century.

2.6 CABINETS 1866 - c 1914

By 1866 sales of cartes de visite had fallen well below the dizzy heights to which they had soared in 1862/3. In an effort to boost flagging profits the London photographer F.R. Window proposed a new card format, larger than the carte, with dimensions measuring 5¾ x 4 inches for the print, 6½ x 4¼ inches for the mount. He named this format the Cabinet card. (See Plate 12) Promoted nationally and internationally by the editor of *The Photographic News*, the Cabinet made only slow progress in the early years, but had established a firm hold on the market in the 1880s and 1890s. It continued in demand throughout the Edwardian period and into World War One. In the post war period, however, the postcard was the most popular format.

PLATE 12. J. BROWN, Providence Place, Ashton Old Road, Openshaw.
Full length standing woman with album. 1860s. Carte de visite. Author's Collection.
ALLEN NIELD, Leeds, Manchester, Stockport, etc.
Standing woman with album. c1901. Cabinet. Author's Collection.
These two portraits illustrate the different dimensions of the carte de visite and cabinet formats. Both are typical of their period. The thin card, square corners, full length standing figure and the backdrop with a receding view through the open archway are all typical features of the 1860s. The thick card mount with gold bevelling and lettering is typical of the 1890s/turn of the century style.

DATING CARD FORMATS

Since the carte de visite and cabinet formats dominated the market in commercial portrait photography for a period of some fifty years, we need to look for ways of assigning more specific dates to individual card photographs. As these photographs are also artefacts, it is important to examine all aspects of their makeup to arrive at a possible date. So, we need to look closely at the physical appearance of the cardboard mount. The trade had to introduce changes in the appearance and design of the card mounts if only to lure customers with the charm of novelty. Of course, though we can often provide firm dates for the introduction of any innovation, we can never determine exactly when it was adopted or dropped by individual photographers. The dating of innovations, however, does give *post quem* dates for individual portraits. We also need to study any written information on the mount, both printed and manuscript, as this too will provide clues to dating. The other factors which can assist in dating are the identification of the photographic process used to produce the portrait, and an ability to identify and interpret the information contained in the image itself.

In attempting to date card photographs within a family collection, it is also important not to look at individual portraits in isolation but to relate them to their neighbours. Portraits emanating from the same studio *may* indicate members of the same family unit. Evidence from the cards within such a group can sometimes give a sequential order of production as explained below. But do be very careful when undertaking such an exercise to return any photographs taken from an album to their original positions. Those of us fortunate enough to inherit an album which retains its original sequencing should take care to preserve the order of the photographs and study it closely. It, too, may provide clues to relationships or suggest connections.

3.1 Card Mount and its Appearance

The first thing to remember when examining a card mounted photograph is that the date of the photograph need not necessarily be contemporary with the mount onto which it is pasted! So, for example, memorial portraits were frequently produced after the death of a relative. These often feature portraits copied from an earlier period and pasted onto a mount of a later design. Having said that, the majority of portraits are contemporary with their mounts and stylistic changes in mount design are helpful pointers in dating. Inevitably some trends are adopted which echo or repeat earlier fashions and this can sometimes cause confusion for the non-specialist. Round or square corners are a case in point. Early cards produced in the 1860s tended to have square corners. These were found to cause damage when inserted into the album pages. So, by the 1870s photographers had the option of using cards with rounded corners and these remained the more popular style throughout the 1870s, 1880s and 1890s. By the turn of the century the fashion reverts back to the square format, though by this time the mounts are much thicker than in the early period. Happily, however, there are some stylistic changes which will help even the most inexperienced make headway with this difficult problem of dating. They include:

3.1.1   Thickness of the Card Mount

This is surprisingly useful in dating since the thickness of the cardboard mount nearly doubled between the 1860s and the 1890s. The card used in the 1860s is noticeably thinner than the card of the 1890s. Simply by arranging your card portraits in order of thickness you arrive at some order in their dating!

3.1.2   Gold Bevelling and Gold Lettering

The increasing thickness of the mounting card encouraged the introduction of bevelled edges, which became popular from c1880 to 1914. These bevelled edges were often finished in silver or gold. A feature of mounts produced in the 1890s and early 1900s is the presence of the photographer's monogrammed initials usually positioned on the front, near the base of the card in the right or left corner. These, too, were picked out in gold or silver.

3.1.3   Colour of the Card Mount

As a general rule paler colours were preferred in the 1860s and 1870s with the bolder dark colours like black, chocolate brown, bottle green and burgundy putting in an appearance in the 1880s and 1890s. But remember, shades of cream remained popular throughout the whole period! In the 1890s and 1900s the surface of the card can display a textured appearance which is quite different to anything used in the earlier period.

3.1.4   Protective Tissue

In the 1880s and 1890s some cartes and cabinets came supplied with a protective covering of tissue paper. This was usually pasted along the top of the back of the mounting card and folded over the face of the photograph to guard it from scratches. (See Plate 13) In most cases the tissue has long since disappeared. It was usually removed when the portrait was placed in the album. However, telltale evidence of its original presence can be found on the back of the mount.

PLATE 13.
One carte de visite showing the protective tissue used to cover the face of the photograph and the back of another carte de visite showing the tell tale mark along the top where the protective tissue was attached.
The protective tissue in this example is illustrated with Japanese style design which also bears a registration mark, both of which suggest a date in the 1880s or 1890s. On Fontaine's card the reference to Platinotype enlargements and a design registration number in the bottom left corner, i.e. 151785 suggest a date in the 1890s.

3.1.5 Chinese/Japanese Decoration on Back of Card Mount

In the 1880s and 1890s Britain was gripped by a mania for Japanese design. Liberty, the exclusive London store, was in the forefront of its promotion. This passion for Japanese style is reflected in the decorative designs which featured on card backs at this same period. (See Plate 14)

PLATE 14. Cartes de visite. Author's Collection.
Decorative designs on the verso of four cartes de visite which reflect the interest in Japanese design which prevailed in the 1880s.

3.1.6 Deckle Edges

A decorative feature in the form of serrated edges or deckle edging made its appearance on card mounts from the late 1890s, but it appears to have become more popular in the early years of the twentieth century.

3.2 Printed Information

Cartes de visite produced in the early years if the 1860s carry little or no printed information either on the front or back of the card mount. Photographers, however, quickly came to realise that this represented a missed opportunity to advertise their products. It soon became standard practice to append details of the photographer's name and address on the base of the front of the mount and on the verso. This information was printed or stamped on the mount. It seems reasonable to assume that the use of a stamp indicates a studio concerned to operate with very low overheads and suggests a price sensitive clientele.

It is also normal to find information on the mount relating to the range of products or services offered by the photographer or references to awards, medals or distinctions that would serve to enhance the reputation of the studio in question. All of these can potentially assist with the dating of the photograph.

3.2.1 Photographer's Name and Address

Armed with this information resort can be made to town trade directories in an attempt to discover the dates when a photographer was resident at a particular address. Few people will need to be reminded of the limitations of the nineteenth century trade directory (irregularity of publication, inaccuracy, and incompleteness) which at best can only offer a guide to approximate dates. That said, trade directories remain a valuable source of information.

Fortunately for our purposes the Royal Photographic Society Historical Group has published a series of lists of nineteenth century photographers compiled from trade directories for a growing number of towns and counties in Britain. Details of these and other similar publications are provided in an appendix at the back of this booklet.

It can prove a worthwhile exercise to look carefully at all the portraits issued by the same studio. It is sometimes possible to arrive at a sequential order for the taking of the photographs as in the illustrated example which documents a change of studio ownership. (See Plate 15) The word "late" is useful in indicating a date close to the change of ownership and if this is not apparent from the trade directories, it will probably have been advertised in the local papers.

PLATE 15. T. BROWN & SAMUEL BETTONEY, Maryport.
c1860s and 1870s. Cartes de visite. Author's Collection.
The information contained on the backs of these cartes de visite gives a chronological sequence for the taking of the photographs.

3.2.2 The Photographic Multiple

The emergence of the multiple store with branches in different towns was an innovative feature of retailing in the nineteenth century. Commercial portrait photography lent itself nicely to this development. Two multiples of the early period are the London School of Photography and the firm of John Burton and Sons. However, the chain store studio became more widespread from the late 1870s. The biggest Victorian photographic multiple was the firm of A & G Taylor whose head office was based in London. Many people will have photographs by this firm in their family collections. At one time A & G Taylor had over 50 branches in Britain together with outlets in America and Paris. Printing was done centrally in London at Forest Hill and the listing of the branches on the back of the mounts can provide a useful clue to dating. See Colin Osman, The Studios of A & G Taylor, *The PhotoHistorian Supplement* No.111 (March 1996). This also has a guide to dating by mount design on page 12.

Taylors' nearest rival was the Liverpool based multiple of Brown, Barnes and Bell. This firm never had more than a dozen branches at any one time, excluding its studios in Liverpool and London. It came into existence in 1876/7. It expanded quickly during the early years of the 1880s but decline soon followed. For dates of branches see Audrey Linkman, Brown, Barnes and Bell, *The PhotoHistorian*, No.111 (March 1996), pp.15-21.

For lists of other local multiples with branch addresses and dates including the firms of James Brown, Eddison Ltd., Hills and Saunders, London School of Photography, Williams & Williams etc., see Audrey Linkman, The Photographic Multiple in the Nineteenth Century, *The PhotoHistorian*, No.110 (January 1996), pp.16-26.

3.2.3   Information on Products and Services

Photographers used the space on the back of their card mounts to advertise awards, products and services which were intended to give them the edge over their rivals. This information can sometimes assist with dating.

Album Portraits

As we know, purpose designed albums were introduced in the early 1860s specifically to promote sales of cartes de visite. In those early days cartes were also known as album portraits. Any reference to album portraits on the carte back indicates a date in the early years of the 1860s.

Awards and Medals

Photographers took great care to print details of any medals, awards, honours or distinctions on the backs of the card mounts. Ambitious photographers entered work at exhibitions and this demonstrated their artistic pretensions. The award of any prize or medal advertised their artistic superiority over fellow photographers and could be used to justify higher charges. Many of these awards include the date of the competition and the latest dated award provides a *post quem* dating for the photograph. Be warned, you may need a magnifying glass to read these dates! (See Plate 16)

PLATE 16. POUNCY, Dorchester.
Vignetted portrait of a little girl. c1865.
Carte de visite. Author's Collection.
The child's doll is just visible on the bottom right of the picture. Everything about this photograph suggests a date in the 1860s. The cream card is delicately thin though unusually for this date edged in gold paint. Square corners and the absence of any printing on the front of the mount confirm an 1860s date. The prize medals represented on the verso date between 1859 and 1865. So a date near to 1865 would seem appropriate.

New Instantaneous Process

The phrase "New Instantaneous Process" often appears printed on the verso of card portraits. The process was usually advertised as being particularly good for child portraits. There was, however, no such process. If the words have any relevance at all they probably refer to the faster gelatine negatives which came into widespread use from c1880. These negatives reduced exposures from seconds to fractions of a second, a considerable advantage when photographing children and animals.

Lighting

Throughout the nineteenth century the majority of studios relied on natural daylight. Daylight conferred the advantage of a free and unlimited supply, but entailed the disadvantages of unreliability and the restriction to working during the hours of daylight. Victorian photographers, therefore, experimented with various forms of artificial lighting and this sometimes featured in the advertising on the backs of cartes and cabinets. These occasional references can assist with dating.

Moule's Photogen 1857 - c1862/3

On 18 February 1857 John Moule of Hackney Road, London took out a patent on an apparatus for burning pyrotechnic compounds for the purposes of illumination. The Photogen comprised a large, glass lantern, which was pierced with holes in its base to admit air and fitted with a pipe at the top to carry off the fumes. A crucible was inserted into the lantern to hold the 'burning composition' which gave off a vivid white light. The exposed plate was either turned into a glass positive or used as a negative from which to strike paper prints. Largely advertised as a means of taking photographs at night, the Photogen did not enjoy extensive or prolonged use. There are references to its employment at the Royal Polytechnic Institution which offered lectures and practical demonstrations in the winter of 1858; in the North Woolwich Gardens; and in a small number of studios in London and the provinces.

Luxograph 1878 - c1886

This was an apparatus for burning pyrotechnic compounds similar to those used in Moule's Photogen. The Luxograph apparatus comprised a burner, a flue to carry of the smoke, a huge concave reflector to throw light onto the sitter, and a diaphanous screen to subdue the intensity of the light. It was the combination of reflectors and screens that constituted the Luxograph, not the nature of the light that was used. The Luxograph appears to have been employed particularly at fancy dress balls where impromptu studios were rigged up in adjoining rooms. Contemporary sources make reference to a 'Luxograph craze' and particular popularity in the winter of 1880-1881. (See Plate 17)

PLATE 17. TURNBULL & SONS,
75 Jamaica Street, Glasgow and 32 Cathcart Street, Greenock.
Threequarter seated male with fob. c1879.
Carte de visite. Author's Collection.
The list of licences noted on the back of this carte suggest that Turnbull & Sons courted a prosperous clientele among the citizens of Glasgow. The appearance of the sitter does nothing to contradict this impression. The reference to the Luxograph also suggests enterprise on the part of the photographers and dates the portrait to the end of the 1870s, possibly early 1880s.

Electric Light 1877 -

Though experiments with electric light and photographic portraiture took place as early as 1863, it was not until 1877 that the first electric light portrait studio was opened at 182, Regent Street, London by an American, Henry Van der Weyde. In the early days of electricity photographers had to acquire and maintain their own generators which was a costly and cumbersome business. This explains why other studios were relatively slow to adopt electricity. By 1882 there were only four studios with electric light in London: Van der Weyde's; the London Stereoscopic Company (probably from 1879); J.E. Mayall in New Bond Street (probably from 1881); and Negretti and Zambra at the Crystal Palace. Real growth in this area had to await the provision of mains electricity in towns and cities, a development which came in the 1890s and later. Manchester's first electric studio came in 1892 at Lafayette's on Deansgate. Therefore, most references to electric light, date a portrait to the 1890s or later.

Studio photographers converted only slowly to the exclusive use of electric lighting. Many continued to employ free and familiar daylight when it was available. In September 1895, Mora, a studio proprietor based in Brighton, wrote to *The Photographic News* stating that he had installed electric lighting some two years previously at a cost of several hundred pounds. The number of sitters had not increased sufficiently even to pay the interest on the outlay; his investment, he concluded, "has been more an advertisement than any substantial benefit."

Gas Light 1879 -

The major difficulty associated with the use of gas in portrait photography was the provision of sufficient intensity of illumination without at the same time creating oppressive heat. P.M. Laws, a studio proprietor of Newcastle upon Tyne, played a prominent role in devising a working method between 1879 and 1881. The introduction of the more sensitive dry plate at this date assisted his efforts. Spasmodic references to the use of gas continue to occur to the end of the century; the gas lamp of Captain Eugene Himley in 1885; the system of Mr Treble of Clapham Junction in 1893; the gas lamp of the Albion Albumenising Company in 1896; the trial studio for incandescent gaslight by O. Sichel & Co. in 1896; and studio lighting by the Atmospheric Gas Company in 1900.

Magnesium Flash Lighting c1886 -

The first portrait by magnesium light was taken as early as 1864 and for the next twenty years the use of magnesium remained largely experimental. During this early period magnesium in the form of wire or ribbon was used, either suspended freely or fed through a purpose-designed lamp. Following a dramatic fall in price in 1886, a number of people began experimenting with magnesium powder looking for a method of getting it to burn instantaneously, evenly and safely. By the late 1880s numerous magnesium flash lamps had appeared on the market. Generally, however, magnesium flash powder was unsuitable for use in the commercial studio. As it burned, it gave off an unpleasant, dense white smoke which lingered in the room; it left particles of dust in the air which dirtied the surfaces on which they settled; and it tended to produce prints with heavy shadows and lacking in delicacy. As a result the use of magnesium flash powder was confined mainly to newspaper photographers and those working in dark situations such as mines and caverns.

Photographic Patents

Throughout the fifty or more years when card portraits dominated the market, photographers constantly sought to introduce novelties in treatment or finish that would re-kindle interest and entice customers into the studio. Some photographers protected their "inventions" by patent and sold the rights, techniques, materials and equipment to fellow photographers. Those who had purchased the right to introduce these innovations were naturally keen to advertise the fact on the backs of their cartes and cabinets. This advertising of licences for the various processes gives a *post quem* date; in most cases it also gives a good approximate date, as many of these processes do not appear to have enjoyed long-term popularity. Photographers who could afford to pay for these licences were unlikely to be those at the cheapest end of the market. (See Plate 17) Examples of these patents and their dates of introduction are listed below:

Sarony Photocrayon (1869 -)

Van der Weyde Patent Process of Finishing Photographs (1872 -)

Ferranti-Turner Patent (1873 -)

Lambertype, Chromotype and Contretype (1875 -)

Mezzotint Vignette (1876 -)

The Patents, Designs and Trade Marks Act of 1883

Following the Act of 1883 card mount manufacturers could register their ownership of decorative designs. The fact that a design had been so registered is sometimes acknowledged on the card back in the tiniest print. Some of these acknowledgements give the registration number. By referring back to the registration numbers in the Board of Trade records we can get a *post quem* dating for the protection of the design used on the card mount. (See Plate 13)

1884 (1 Jan 84 - 29 Dec 84)	1 - 19661
1885 (29 Dec 84 - 21 Dec 85)	19662 - 39954
1886 (21 Dec 85 - 20 Dec 86)	39955 - 63796
1887 (20 Dec 86 - 21 Dec 87)	63797 - 89956
1888 (21 Dec 87 - 28 Dec 88)	89957 - 116465
1889 (28 Dec 88 - 21 Dec 89)	116466 - 140961

Copyright

Some cartes and cabinets carry the words 'Entered at Stationers' Hall', or variations to that effect. This phrase indicates that the photographer has sought to register copyright in the photograph.

On 29 July 1862 the Fine Art Copyright Act (Victoria 25 and 26, Cap. 68) passed into law. This was the first copyright act specifically to include photographs. By its terms no copyright was secured until registration was completed in the approved manner at Stationers' Hall. This involved the filing of an official form, usually (though not obligatorily) accompanied by a copy of the photograph in question, together with payment of a registration fee - set at one shilling per entry in 1862.

Those original forms plus any attached photographs are preserved today in the Public Record Office at Kew. The collection is arranged in order of date of registration: there is no corresponding photographer index. So, while this splendid collection will provide a precise date for a registered photograph, you do need to know the date before you can access the collection!

Photographers would only normally seek to register photographs which they were intending to publish and reproduce in quantity for commercial sales. These included portraits of celebrities, both local and national, and landscape or architectural views which sold to the tourist trade. Many portraits of celebrities carry no identification so the wording 'Entered at Stationers' Hall' can indicate that this is no ordinary family photograph.

3.3 Manuscript Information

Sadly manuscript information is the exception rather than the rule on most Victorian family photographs. The manuscript information that does appear can take a number of forms. Sometimes we simply have a name; sometimes the name is accompanied by a date. In the case of children, in particular, the name can be accompanied by details of age or date of birth. We should always bear in mind that photographs were regularly exchanged between friends and that a date may refer to the date of the gift rather than the time of the actual sitting. The inclusion of the word "Taken" can be very reassuring on this point! It was not unusual for a portrait to be converted to a memorial portrait by the addition of a manuscript note indicating that the subject of the photograph had subsequently died or "entered into rest". (See Plate 18)

PLATE 18.
JOHN LANCASTER, Grosvenor Street, Chester and 6 Price Street, Birkenhead.
Maria Thorpe. c1873. Carte de visite. Author's Collection.
The advertising on the verso of this photograph together with the manuscript information give a
reasonably tight date for the portrait. Lancaster is advertising the new Cameo Vignette portrait which
we know came onto the market in 1871.
The manuscript information written in an authentic script reads: Maria Thorpe my Cousin died 1875.
The photograph must therefore have been taken between 1871 and 1875.

The date of death is usually given in such cases, sometimes accompanied by the date of birth and suitable verses or quotations from the Bible. Take note whether the hand writing is contemporary or of a later date. Information supplied by a later generation may be more suspect. Be warned, even the most seemingly reliable dating can turn out to be inaccurate or misleading.

However, it was not only the owners of the photographs who made notes in manuscript on their photographs. Sometimes photographers did, too! Photographers' notes usually take the form of a number written in manuscript on the back of a portrait. This is the reference number to the negative which was preserved in store for a number of years in the hope of after orders. Here again by studying these reference numbers from the same studio we can get a sequential order for the taking of the photographs. (See Plate 19)

PLATE 19. PERCY MITCHELL, Sydenham, London.
Cartes de visite. Author's Collection.

Both cartes were issued from the same studio and both carry a studio reference number. Assuming that no. 22376 was produced before no. 26545 we have a chronological sequence for two cartes. If the manuscript information on 22376, i.e. "N S B Dec/80" refers to the date of production or thereabout, we can feel justified in dating the boy with the whip to the early years of the 1880s, perhaps c1882.

Occasionally, too, the back of a card portrait carries a label or manuscript instructions which reveal that an order has been placed for an enlargement to be made of the photograph in question; or which give brief directions to the colour artist. Both of these indicate that the portrait held special significance for its owner as colouring and enlargements entailed additional expense.

3.4 Photographic Processes

Albumen Prints

Throughout the 1850s the highest class of photographer spurned the collodion positive seeing it merely as a cut-price, inferior daguerreotype. They concentrated their energies instead on perfecting the printing of paper positives from the collodion glass negatives. Thin plain paper was coated with a layer of egg white (albumen) containing salt and sensitised with a silver nitrate solution before use. The paper was then usually contact printed under the collodion negative using daylight. The majority of paper prints produced from the 1850s to 1880 are albumen prints.

Gelatin Prints

Albumen printing continued in operation until c1878 when commercially produced, cheap, reliable, ready made gelatin dry plate negatives became available over the counter. Since gelatin plate negatives were considerably more sensitive, collodion rapidly went out of widespread, general use. The process introduced for gelatin negatives was soon applied to printing papers. Silver bromide papers came into general use from c1880 and have remained in use ever since. Less sensitive silver chloride papers appeared at the same time. For the remainder of the century photographers enjoyed such an extensive range of options with regard to papers, processes, toning and finishing that identification becomes a matter for the trained specialist.

Since process identification is a particularly specialised sphere, readers are referred to Brian Coe and Mark Haworth-Booth, *A Guide to Early Photographic Processes*, Victoria and Albert Museum (1983). The National Museum of Photography, Film and Television at Bradford have put time and effort into producing a publication on the subject of processes, but this seems to be in abeyance at the time of writing.

Carbon Prints

A variety of other processes were sometimes employed and these can assist in dating. A practical carbon printing process was invented by Joseph Wilson Swan in 1864. Whereas silver prints were liable to fade over time, carbon had the advantage of permanence. However it was a difficult process to work and its use in the portrait studio centred mainly on good quality, framed enlargements. Its application to small work i.e. cartes and cabinets followed a visit to this country in 1875 and 1876 by the Frenchman, Claude Léon Lambert, specifically to promote his invention, the chromotype. Chromotypes are cartes de visite made by the carbon process. Chromotypes were difficult to produce and photographers had to purchase a licence costing in the region of twenty pounds which gave them exclusive rights for a particular district. Chromotypes were therefore expensive and only offered by leading photographers. Because of their complexity they enjoyed only a short life, most being produced between 1875 and c1880, though Jabez Hughes of Ryde on the Isle of Wight continued to produce carbon work until his death in 1884. Chromotypes have a distinctive appearance. They are purplish brown in colour; the photographer's details appear as part of the photograph, and the words "patent" or "permanent chromotype" usually feature on the face of the print. (See Plate 20) For more information about carbon in the commercial studio, see: Audrey Linkman, The Stigma of Instability: The Carbon Process and Commercial Photography in Britain, 1864 to 1880, *Photographica World*, No.91 (Winter 1999/2000), pp.8-32.

Platinum Prints

Platinum was another permanent process, which was patented in 1873 and refined for practical use by 1880. It became more popular from the late 1880s attracting the attention of art photographers and pictorialists. It was introduced into commercial portrait work only by the more exclusive studios whose customers could afford the prices charged. Unfortunately the use of platinum in photography coincided with steep rises in price which effectively ended the production of platinotypes by the First World War. Platinotypes which are stored in albums can sometimes leave rust-coloured impressions on a facing page. This effect is caused by residual iron salts leeching from the platinum paper.

Portraits on Opal Glass

Portraits on opal glass were produced from the early 1860s and continued throughout the century and after. The majority of opalotypes were framed for hanging on walls, or intended for display on stands etc. For further information see: Audrey Linkman, Flashed, Pot and Porcelain: The Opalotype in Victorian Britain, *Photographica World*, Nos. 80 & 81 (March and June 1997).

3.5 Image Content

The photograph itself may contain important evidence, which, taken in conjunction with the other elements, will contribute towards a possible dating.

3.5.1 Costume and Fashion

Clearly one important source for dating portraits is the dress of the sitter. Sadly, however, even for the expert costume specialist this can never be an exact science. While they can often supply dates for the emergence of a particular fashion

PLATE 20. J. PATON, Greenock.
Baby in armchair. c1877. Chromotype. Author's Collection.
Most chromotypes are easy to recognise and most can be dated to the second half of the 1870s.
The word chromotype usually appears on the photograph (as is the case here) and the photographer's
name and address are usually, though not always, an integral part of the photograph - not printed
separately on the mount as in standard practice. Chromotypes have a glossy finish and a distinctive
rich purple brown colour. Carbon prints, like this, are permanent, i.e. they do not fade. Chromotypes
were more expensive than other cartes de visite so we could expect this to be the child of parents who
enjoyed a comfortable income.

or style, costume historians can rarely give precise dates for its appearance in a photograph. In dating dress experts have to take into account the financial circumstances, level of fashion consciousness, age and sex of the wearer. And in the case of unidentified sitters, this can only be conjectural.

Male dress is notoriously more difficult to date than female dress. And in some portraits, notably the popular vignette style (head and shoulders only, merging softly into a plain background), very little of the dress appears in the photograph anyway.

Any detailed account of changes in fashion in the Victorian period is beyond the scope of this publication. A reading list on this topic is supplied in an appendix at the end of the booklet.

3.5.2 Studio Accessories

Throughout the Victorian period commercial photographers regularly used painted backdrops in their portrait work. These backdrops were intended to provide an anonymous setting for the sitter, yet one which implied financial security and high social status. The drawing room interior and the outdoor parkland setting persisted throughout the period. Certain backdrops were popular at particular periods. Backdrops which featured receding views, for example, tend to fall out of favour after the 1860s.

Props and accessories were introduced to help support the make believe world of the backdrop: the balustrade or rustic seat in outdoor settings, the table, chair and plant in drawing room interiors. Only props which were thought to enhance the sitter's prestige were allowed into the portrait. While the majority of objects in the portraits are undoubtedly conventional studio props, sitters on occasion did introduce items of personal value whose presence in the picture can be a significant clue to the reason for the taking of the portrait. Certain studio props became particularly fashionable at particular periods:

The bicycle - an article in *The Photographic News* in July 1896 refers to the novelty of keeping bicycles as studio accessories especially for the use of young ladies who were then saved the necessity of bringing their own machines with them.

The masthead - an article in *The Photographic News* in the summer of 1882 recommends the effective use of the masthead with young boys in sailor suits. (See Plate 21)

The swing was fashionable in the early years of the 1880s, especially for young ladies.

PLATE 21. ROBERT WHITEHOUSE, 59 Piccadilly, Manchester.
Young boy posing on masthead accessory. 1890s.
Cabinet. Documentary Photography Archive, Manchester D50/2/137.
If the masthead came into fashion in the 1880s it was clearly still in use in the 1890s. The Manchester
trade directories list Whitehouse at this address between 1890 and 1897. The dark green mount, gold
lettering and monogram are also typical of the 1890s.

3.5.3 Naked Babies

While naked babies feature in Victorian art photography, few Victorian infants ever appeared before the commercial camera other than fully clothed. The 1890s saw the beginning of change with the children of the rich revealing bare feet and ankles, or wearing little off-the-shoulder shifts. The baby lying naked on the rug or sitting on its mother's knee only became popular in the twentieth century.

3.5.4 Celebrations and Special Occasions

The Victorian public visited the photographer's studio to celebrate a special occasion or to record in some way an event which enhanced the family's status and standing. Our ancestors visited the photographer's studio to celebrate rites of passage, such as christenings, breechings, comings of age, engagements, weddings, anniversaries etc. Christenings can usually be identified by the elaborate, long robe traditional to the occasion. Less obviously apparent are the youth wearing his first pair of long trousers, or the young girl advertising her adult status by putting her hair up and letting her skirts down. A man and a woman photographed together in the photographer's studio may be celebrating their marriage or engagement. To be photographed together was tantamount to a statement of intent! Only very rich Victorian brides wore white. Most women wore the best day dress they could afford. Look closely at every detail. Get out the magnifying glass. Note any rings on a woman's finger. Is there a flower in the man's buttonhole? Look, too, for matching portraits intended to face each other in the album, the lady on one page, the gentleman on the other. These occur regularly in the case of engagements, weddings and anniversaries. Anniversary photographs may show the couple individually as just described, or photographed together, or surrounded by their immediate family. Even the final rite of passage, death itself, is frequently celebrated in the Victorian family album.

The ability to be able to identify the occasion behind the photograph plays a crucial role in enabling us to unravel the mysteries of our Victorian Family Photographs. If the identity of the sitter is known, and the occasion of the portrait can be identified as the wedding or engagement photograph, then this will give genealogists who know the family history a firm dating for the photograph. Conversely, if we have an approximate date for a portrait and know the occasion which is being celebrated we can look for family members whose lives fit those events and begin to assign possible identities to the unknown subjects of our family photographs. Identifying these rites and celebrations will form the subject matter of another publication in this series.

ℬIBLIOGRAPHY

History of Photography

Brian COE, *The Birth of Photography: The Story of the Formative Years*, Ash & Grant (1976).

Helmut & Alison GERNSHEIM, *The History of Photography*, Thames & Hudson (1969).

Helmut GERNSHEIM, *The Rise of Photography 1850 - 1880: The Age of Collodion*, Thames & Hudson (1988).

Audrey LINKMAN, *The Victorians: Photographic Portraits*, Tauris Parke (1993).

B.E.C. Howarth LOOMES, *Victorian Photography: A Collector's Guide*, Ward Lock (1974).

Don STEEL & Lawrence TAYLOR, *Family History in Focus*, Lutterworth (1984).

Books on Fashion

Madeleine GINSBURG, *Victorian Dress in Photographs*, Batsford (1982).

Avril LANSDELL, *Fashion à la Carte 1860-1900: A study of fashion through cartes de visite*, Shire ((1985).

Fashion in Photographs. A series published by Batsford in association with the National Portrait Gallery

Miles LAMBERT, *Fashion In Photographs 1860-1880*, Batsford (1991).

Sarah LEVITT, *Fashion In Photographs 1880-1900*, Batsford (1991).

Katrina ROLLEY, *Fashion In Photographs 1900-1920*, Batsford (1992).

Elizabeth OWEN, *Fashion In Photographs 1920-1940*, Batsford (1993).

Published Lists of Photographers

The Royal Photographic Society Historical Group periodically issues Supplements which list, with dates and addresses, all the photographers in a town or county whose names appeared in the local trade directories. These lists can be used in conjunction with a photographer's name and address on the backs of card photographs to fix approximate dates. A list of available Supplements can be obtained from the Publications Secretary of the RPS Historical Group.

There are also a number of independent publications which contain similar (and often more detailed) information.

ENGLAND

Cornwall Charles THOMAS, *Views and Likenesses: Early photographers and their work in Cornwall and the Isles of Scilly 1839 - 1870*, Truro, Royal Institution of Cornwall (1988).

Doncaster Keith I P ADAMSON, *Photographers in Victorian Doncaster 1842 - 1900*, Doncaster Museum Service (1998).

Hertfordshire Bill SMITH, *Hertfordshire Photographers 1839 - 1939*. Available from Bill Smith, 344 Grace Way, Stevenage, SG1 5AP

Hampshire Martin NORGATE, *Directory of Hampshire Photographers 1850-1969*. Hampshire County Council, Museums Service (1995).

London Michael PRITCHARD, *A Directory of London Photographers 1841 - 1908*. Rev ed., Watford, PhotoResearch (1994).

Manchester Audrey LINKMAN, *Manchester Photographers 1901 - 1939*. Available from Audrey Linkman, D.P.A., C/o 7 Towncroft Lane, Bolton, BL1 5EW. £2.00p (p & p £2.50)

Scarborough	Anne & Paul BAYLISS, *Photographers in Mid-Nineteenth Century Scarborough.*

Scarborough   Anne & Paul BAYLISS, *Photographers in Mid-Nineteenth Century Scarborough.*
Available from A. M. Bayliss, Flat 5, 12 Esplanade, Scarborough, YO11 2AF. £4.50.

Warrington   David FORREST, *Warrington Photographers 1854 - 1992.* Liverpool & S.W. Lancashire FHS (1993)
Available from J.D. Griffiths, 9 Manor Road, Lymm, WA13 OAY.

Wiltshire   Martin NORGATE et al., *Photographers in Wiltshire 1842-1939,* Wiltshire Library & Museum Service (1985) Wiltshire Monograph No.5.

York   Hugh MURRAY *Photographs and photographers of York: The early years 1844-1879,* Yorkshire Architectural & York Archaeological Society (1986)

IRELAND

Edward CHANDLER, Early Irish Pioneers, *The PhotoHistorian* No.92 (Spring 1991), pp.20-28.

A. D. MORRISON-LOW, *A Brief Survey of Nineteenth Century Photography in Ireland,* in Michael Pritchard (editor), *Birth and Early Technology and Art: The Years of Photography,* RPS Historical Group, Bath.

SCOTLAND

Sara STEVENSON & A. D. MORRISON-LOW, *Scottish Photography: A Bibliography 1839-1939,* Salvia Books & Scottish Society for the History of Photography, (1990). Includes references to individual photographers.

Paisley   Don McCOO, *Paisley Photographers 1850-1900,* Foulis Archive Press, Paisley (1986).

Also Available

CARING FOR YOUR FAMILY PHOTOGRAPHS AT HOME

By Audrey Linkman

£3.75 (p&p 50p extra)

Forthcoming

RITES AND CELEBRATIONS

Interpreting Victorian Studio Portraits

By Audrey Linkman

OUTDOOR PORTRAITS

Itinerant Photographers in the Nineteenth Century

By Audrey Linkman